Help Us:
Prayers of The Rev. Fleming Rutledge

Compiled and edited by Rev. Jason Micheli

Foreward by Rev. Teer Hardy

A Publication of Crackers and Grape Juice

crackersandgrapejuice.com

Copyright © Crackers and Grape Juice
Edited by Jason Micheli

Table of Contents

Foreward

The Word Still Speaks: On the Prayers of Fleming Rutledge
By Rev. Teer Hardy

There's a danger in writing forewards like this. You can end up sounding like you are handing out a lifetime achievement award, or worse, offering a eulogy for someone who is very much still preaching, teaching, and correcting the Church with more gospel clarity than most of us dare to attempt.

So let me just say this: Fleming Rutledge changed my preaching. Not because I wanted to be a better speaker or needed more literary illustrations to impress the pew, but because I finally heard what it sounds like when the Word of God is proclaimed without apology, sentimentality, or self-help strategies masquerading as grace.

Fleming taught me to stop writing "Let us" sermons. You know the ones: "Let us be more generous," "Let us love more boldly," "Let us live into resurrection." On the surface, these statements sound like an invitation. They can be inspirational but end up as another version of the law, placing the burden back on the hearer to accomplish what only God can do. Fleming's preaching and prayers refuse to let us get away with that. She does not give us a checklist. She gives us Christ. Crucified. Risen. Coming again. She gives us a promise.

This collection of prayers is soaked in that same Christ-centered conviction. These are not performative petitions or polite liturgical filler. Each one was spoken spontaneously—without script or rehearsal—at the end of a podcast episode, and yet they reveal the depth of Fleming's personal faith and theological conviction. These are the prayers of someone who trusts that God is not just listening but acting. Consider the prayer that cries out:

"Dear Lord, we don't know how to say what you want us to say... But you know, and it's your will, to speak through the most unexpected people at the most unexpected times" (Episode 121).

That is a word for every preacher who has stared down a pulpit with nothing but a blank page and a desperate hope that the Spirit will show up.

Or take this, a benediction disguised as lament:

"Oh Lord, let us never forget that we are part of the problem… Save us from ourselves over and over and over again, as you have always done" (Episode 95).

Fleming does not flatter the Church; she intercedes for it. And as one who has spent more time in the pulpit because of her encouragement, I can testify that these prayers are a gift for preachers and anyone clinging to the hope that the gospel is true.

Even her prayers for the nation refuse to traffic in cheap civic religion:

"Do not let the hope of the world in the United States become lost. Please do not let the Statue of Liberty's torch become meaningless" (Episode 51).

These are not abstract theological meditations. These are honest prayers offered for real people in real pain. Her voice is both prophetic and pastoral, unafraid to name the darkness but even more insistent on proclaiming the light:

"Make us citizens of that kingdom, Lord… Turn our face to the light, the light that comes at the end of all time… the hope that places all its resources in the promises that you have made to us in your beloved Son" (Episode 185).

To read these prayers is to overhear a preacher who *actually* believes this stuff. And more than that, someone who trusts that God is still at work in pulpits, pews, podcasts, and even in people like you and me.

So if you are looking for a collection of eloquent sentiments, you may be disappointed. But if you want to encounter the living God, through the trembling voice of one of his most faithful heralds, listen closely.

Fleming is still preaching. Thanks be to God.

Soli Deo Gloria

Eastertide 2025

"Straighten out our beloved country"

"Dear Heavenly Father, please, by the power of your Spirit, give the three of us the strength that we need to continue to preach the Gospel of Jesus Christ and Him crucified to an unheeding, deeply confused, and ignorant world. I pray especially for these two young men who will carry forward the work of all those who have gone before. Thanks be to God. And Lord, please, give your healing powers and graces to Jason. In the name of Christ, we ask all these things and all the things that we are too ignorant or too lazy to say. And bless and keep and guide and straighten out our beloved country, we beseech you. In the name of the Father, and of the Son, and of the Holy Spirit. Amen."

— Episode 9&10

"Promised to us in the resurrection of Jesus Christ"

"Come, Holy Spirit, dwell with the four of us at this moment and with all who might be listening. Move upon our hearts with all the power that called the creation into being, with the power that raised Jesus from the dead, and with the power that sent a group of very unlikely disciples into the world carrying the living, flaming, breathing Word of God. Grant to us, and to all who hear this podcast, a sense of your purpose for the world. For the individual people whom you call to yourself to carry this promise of unquenchable power for the overcoming of sin and the final conquest and victory over death promised to us in the resurrection of Jesus Christ, our Lord, in whose name we pray. Amen."

— Episode 15

"Give us that faith"

"Let's ask the Lord to take away our self-consciousness...

O Lord our God, heavenly Father, great Creator, Father of our Lord and Savior Jesus Christ, teach us again, and again, that this is your word to us, that it is not only your gigantic voice of command that parted the waters, but your intimate whispers to us, calling our names, setting us in our place, making the ground firm under our feet as we navigate the troubled waters of our world, never more so than now.

Make that ground firm under our feet as we listen to your voice, speaking to us through the pages of this, your Word of God written. Help us to listen for your voice and to set aside the voices of others who disbelieve, cast dispersions, mock, undermine our faith. Help us to find the right places to look for the fathers and mothers of the faith who read the Scripture with awe and wonder.

Give us that faith, Lord, again and again.

Give us the ears of little Samuel and the humility of the prophets who knew they

could not do in themselves what they were
called to do. Let us hear your Word. Amen."

— Episode 43

"Help us"

"Lord Jesus Christ, help us to remember that you sought out precisely the people who everyone else wanted to exclude. But you called out the most surprising people. You called Zacchaeus down from the tree. Please call that part of Zacchaeus and all of us down from our trees, and make us whole.

Raise us up when we fall. Shatter our pride.

Show us whom you want us to serve.

Console and encourage us who are members of congregations as we build up one another in love, according to your promise.

Help us not to seek our own aggrandizement even as we seek to do good.

Help us to be self-forgetful.

Help us to put ourselves in the shoes and hearts of others.

Oh Lord, do not let our country slip away from its foundation. Its firm foundation.

Do not let the hope of the world in the United States become lost.

Please do not let the Statue of Liberty's torch become meaningless.

Please, Lord, for this city, this nation, does bear your name. Oh, Lord, hear. Oh, Lord, forgive.

Oh, Lord, listen and act.

For we, your people, are called by your name.

In the name of the Father, Son, and Holy Spirit."

— Episode 51

"New way of speaking"

"It is my hope and prayer that the Lord quakes all of the pulpits across this land this Sunday, that we might let the Lord do something through us and instead of us trying to change the Lord. Amen to that prayer. I don't think I can say anything that would be more powerful, but dear Lord, I'm so grateful for knowing brothers and sisters through this strange new medium that brings so many blessings and so many curses. Help us Lord to navigate through these deep waters. Modernity is swallowing us up in some ways. Our hearts ache for the young people who have devices to entertain them all the time, and parents who don't talk to them because they're on devices too. Dear Lord, teach us to listen to you, to read your Word, to read, mark, learn, and inwardly digest the Gospel, so that all the preachers all over the country, using every conceivable kind of new way of speaking, way of presenting, grant that through all this confusion and uncertainty and temptation, that we might cleave to the Word, and be cleft by it."

— Episode 53

"With awe and wonder"

"Almighty God, creator of the universe, creator of the stars, sun, moon, planets, galaxies, infinite reaches that we cannot even conceive of.

Grant that we may be mindful of the way in which you came to earth.

Emptying yourself, Lord Jesus, of all your glory, all your power, all your imperial reign, your majesty, leaving it all behind you, entering into our corrupted, polluted, tragic life, the life of Adam, fallen. Let us, let us remember this with awe and wonder, the awe and wonder of children, little children, and with the awe and wonder of the adult who has passed through the time of unbelief and skepticism and come out into the glorious wonder of your gospel truth.

Lord, in this time in our country, when truth and falsehood and fantasy and self-seeking and self-gratification and heedlessness and anger and sometimes real hate, but also fear, a time in which fear seems to predominate among us. Lord, work a miracle for us this Christmas, let large numbers of Christian believers see what you have done for us, what you are doing in us and through us, and

what you will do in your coming again.
Please, Lord, help the church to resist the
fear, the lies, the BS, help us to resist evil,
help us to resist intolerance, help us to resist
indifference.

Please, Lord, call the international
community to account for the Syrian
refugees. Teach us what to do about helpless
people who seek our shores. Help us not to
be defeated and discouraged.

And weary and give up.

Strengthen and confirm God and direct all
those Christians around the world who are
already serving in humility, in sacrifice, in
dedication to those who are suffering in the
most extreme way. And through them, Lord,
glorify the name of our Lord Jesus Christ
and call more of us, many, many more of us,
to the service of this terribly suffering world.

Free us from fear, Lord. Keep us focused on
the star ahead of us. The light, which is the
Word of God, in the beginning, the Word
made flesh, dwelling among us, full of grace
and truth, in His precious and glorious
name, we pray. Amen."

"As you have always done"

"Oh, Lord, let us never forget that we are part of the problem and that my prescriptions and notions about what the church ought to do are just as wrong as everybody else's.

And I beseech you, Lord, that you would save us from ourselves over and over and over again, as you have always done. That you would not abandon us in our sinful presumptions, but that you would continue to work through us in spite of ourselves. As you have always done, stay with us, Lord.

If the evening of the established church is at hand, all we need to do is to ask you to stay with us, to abide with us, to be the true vine. The true vine of which we are actually branches, incredible as that may seem.

If it is true, Lord, that as you say, that we are the branches of your vine, and that you yourself are the vine, then the church does have a life that is not its own, that can never be defeated. And so I pray today, Jason and I pray, and all those who are listening and participating, pray, O Lord, that you would defend, strengthen, and sanctify. Amen."

— Episode 95

"A word on target"

"Dear Lord, we don't know how to say what you want us to say. We don't know how to reach that other person. We are impotent. We do not know how to pray.

Very few of us, Lord, have those gifts of speaking to people who are hostile or bored or indifferent or who think Christian faith is ridiculous. We don't know how to talk to them. But you know, and it's your will, to speak through the most unexpected people at the most unexpected times.

Grant to the members of your family the grace of the Holy Spirit that we may, against our own expectations, speak a word on target to those who seek you and even to those who are not seeking you, Lord, even those within our own family.

Come, Holy Spirit, give us that which we do not have, the tongue to speak your word and to utter your promises to our great good and to your great glory through Jesus Christ our Lord. Amen."

— Episode 121

"With you"

"I would like to read to you the Great
Advent Prayer...

This is the prayer that everyone in my
tradition grew up with during Advent. We
used to read it every Sunday in Advent, and
at all the weekday services too. I don't know
why they changed that, and I wish they
hadn't because hearing it every Sunday and
every evening prayer and every morning
prayer, you memorize it.

Let us pray. Almighty God, give us grace to
cast away the works of darkness and put on
the armor of light. Now in the time of this
mortal life in which Your Son Jesus Christ
came to visit us in great humility, that in the
last day when He shall come again in His
glorious majesty to judge both the living and
the dead, we may rise to the life immortal,
through Him who lives and reigns with You
and the Holy Spirit, one God, now and
forever.

And, O Lord, on this day, as many people
hear these words, grant to us the power to
discern Your works in the midst of us and to
go where You are, where You are, on the
frontier between Satan and all his works and

the oncoming future of the God who is able. In His name, God, Father, Son and Holy Spirit, we pray. Amen."

— Episode 181 & 182

"Hope that is beyond hope"

"Oh God, our Heavenly Father, we come before you in this latter part of the Advent season, knowing ourselves to be enslaved by sin and by the powers of death. Except, O Lord, for the great big "But!" We were enslaved by sin and death, BUT NOW we are no longer slaves, but free, free in our knowledge of the future of your son and his kingdom.

Make us citizens of that kingdom, Lord. Take hold of us in our darkness, in our fear, in our culpability, our mutual culpability. Take hold of us, Lord.

Turn our face to the light, the light that comes at the end of all time and all that is, to remake your entire creation into a new order, a new order of love, grace, mercy, transformation and eternal citizenship in your presence. Lord, make the city of God so real to us that we can slog through our days with what Christians call hope, the hope that is beyond hope, the hope that places all its resources in the promises that you have made to us in your beloved Son.

Grant, Lord, that we may not fear to look at the darkness and take hope in You."

— Episode 185

"Look with mercy"

"Let us pray. O Lord God, our Creator, our Creator, Redeemer, Sustainer, Father, Son, Holy Spirit, hear us when we feebly call upon you out of our manifold sins and wickednesses, avarice, failures, cowardice, bewilderment. Lord, we turn to you and call upon you because we know that is what you want from us.

You love nothing more than to hear the confession of confused, troubled, insecure, worn down people who desire to be your servants. Because you have called us to be your servants, dear Lord, we know that you will give us the strength to do what you have purposed for us to do. Just please, Lord, please keep us faithful to that calling.

Heavenly Father, look with mercy and grace upon your church, riven in a hundred different directions, filled with sin, disgraced by scandal, not just the Catholics, but the Protestants also, and all churches. We all have our besetting difficulties and violations of your commandments, neglect of the gospel. Lord, look mercifully upon your church, which you have called to yourself, and which in spite of our utter inability, you have strengthened, which you have undergirded and overarched with your Spirit. We pray for all those young people who are drawn to faith in our Lord Jesus Christ that you would strengthen them in the midst of this hostile culture, that you would give them courage and joy of a sort that is very different from the joy that the world foolishly promises. Let us seek our being, our past, our present, and our future in you, dear Lord, and in your Son Jesus Christ, in whose name alone is salvation, power, mercy and everlasting love. In his name, we pray, Amen."

— Episode 244

"Vanquished our adversary"

"Almighty and most merciful God, these days we are a fearful people. And if we're not a little bit fearful, then we're not facing reality. And so we pray that you would enable us to face reality, human reality, and the reality of an enemy who wants to undo everything you have done.

In our knowledge of this ruler of this world, who has taken advantage of our fall, this adversary who has been set against you almost but not quite from the beginning.

That you have already come onto the field of battle and vanquished our adversary, leaving him with his rearguard actions, but arming us with faith and with hope. Let us wear this armor, dear Lord. Not the armor of foolish optimism and careless heedlessness, but with the armor that you have given us by your Spirit and through your Word, that we may partake of your sacraments in these reduced and truncated circumstances, with full knowledge that no disease and not even the greatest of sins has any chance against your redemptive purpose in our Lord Jesus Christ. In His name we pray, Amen."

— Episode 270

"Wonders of your love"

"Thank you, dear Lord.

Thank you, Lord Jesus, for these promises, for these assurances. For these, it's not just an invitation, it's an assurance, Lord. I hear you making your voice known to all who will listen, and sometimes to people who won't listen, because you have that power.

Come close to us. Shake us out of our disbelief, our lethargy, our depression. Bring us, O Lord, into your light, and let the festivities of the season point us to you, to your glory, the glories of your righteousness and wonders of your love.

Let us know you, Lord Jesus. Love you, come to you, seek you, and find you. In the name of the Father, and of the Son, and of the Holy Spirit.

Amen. Amen."

— Episode 337

"Exists in your future"

"Heavenly Father, look with mercy and grace upon your church... we all have our besetting difficulties and violations of your commandments... We need an invigorating breath of the Holy Spirit, dear Lord, for your church – all your churches – and for the great church which exists in your future... Let us seek our being – our past, our present, and our future – in you, dear Lord, and in your son Jesus Christ, in whose name, alone, is salvation, power, mercy, and everlasting love. In His name we pray, Amen."

— Episode 344

"Give us grace"

"Heavenly Father, Creator and Lord of the Universe, this whole planet that you have made for your creatures to live on is in anguish, anguish because of the pandemic, anguish because of inequality, anguish because of poverty and hunger, anguish because of what has happened to our water, our air, our living things, the threat that lies over us. Lord, there is so much need and so much fear, and people are reacting more and more. Out of instinct, out of base instinct, the best of us, as well as what we might consider to be the worst of us.

We know that before you, there is no best and worst. There is just a world of sinners needing salvation. Lord, we know that you have the power to raise up leaders and to put down leaders, and we don't understand your ways.

Sometimes it's clear that you have raised someone up. Sometimes, not often, it seems clear that you have cast down someone who was creating harm, and yet so often they seem to live to survive and die in their beds. We don't understand, Lord, what you are up to.

What we do have, Lord, is your word, your living word, which teaches us every day who you are, and the majesty and dominion of your power and of your mercy.

We have this living word to which we may go every day for living water and food for eternal life. And Lord, we also have your son, your son who is himself the living word. Let us who are preachers and teachers and witnesses give testimony to his life that Jesus is not dead, that Jesus is alive, he is alive now.

He is still in the midst of us. We can still be his disciples even as we fear what lies ahead. We need to be your disciples more than ever, Lord, in our country.

We need to be models. We don't need to be angry bigoted devices, bombastic creatures. We need to be your disciples following your path of strength, strength that does not damage, strength that does not put people down, strength that heals, strength that uplifts, strength that cures, strength that redeems, strength that saves.

That, Lord, is your son for us. Please pour into the hearts of your people, those whom you have chosen to be your people, the kind of love that Jesus had for the entire human race, the best that's in us and the worst that's in us. As this Advent season approaches, teach us what it means to live on the frontier, the frontier of the ages where Jesus died, where the power of God is at war with the power of the adversary, and the battlefield, as Dostoevsky wrote, is the heart of man, the hearts of human beings.

Lord, let that battle be won over and over and over in our daily lives by your strength, by your power, by your Holy Spirit, your life-giving, love-giving, recreating, saving Holy Spirit. Lord, we do not know what will happen on Tuesday. We do take heart that so many people in the United States have turned out to vote.

Apparently, with cheerful hearts and pride and gratitude, we don't yet know what that means. Lord, let it mean something good for our whole population, not just for those on one side or the other, but for everyone. We particularly beseech you, Lord, to teach us how to quell this violence, how to reform our much-needed police.

Not throw bottles at them, but help them to see that they need to overhaul the way that they interact with our citizens. Let us all be citizens together. And let those who take this opportunity to riot and loot be given some measure of your Holy Spirit that they may see that destruction accomplishes nothing.

That building, building up, is what will accomplish a truly great country. Each country has its own special gift from you. Each country has traditions, wells of wisdom and even love to draw upon.

"Let us, Lord, do that instead of seeking the bottom all the time. The worst, truly there is no health in us, but you, O Lord, are the one always to have mercy. And most important, those of us on the frontier, looking to you, see ahead of us, not a human built future, but the Kingdom of God, the Kingdom of Heaven, which cannot be defeated, cannot be destroyed, cannot be polluted, cannot be bombed, an eternal city prepared by you for your people, for the nations, with all their treasures brought into it.

Hold us, Lord. Strengthen us. Encourage us.

Give us grace to continue in the path that you have laid for each one of us and all of us together. Have mercy on your suffering church. And I ask, Lord, in particular, a blessing on all those pastors whom I have met in various ways, mostly through social media, but blessedly sometimes in person.

Lord, Lord Jesus, walk with them. Shine the light of your countenance upon us all."

— Election Day 2020

The LORD Sees Not as Man Sees

Samuel 16
Romans 9-11
Fourth Sunday in Lent — 2020

The following prayer and sermon were shared extemporaneously by Rev. Rutledge during a Bible study, just days before our lives were turned upside down by COVID-19.

"Almighty God, Heavenly Father, gather your people together on this fearful day when the virus seems to be taking hold of our nation and its people. We pray to you as the Lord of creation, the savior and preserver of humanity, to God us through this darkness, to give us courage and loving kindness, hope and faith that you alone in the end are the ruler of all things and that even now, your grace, your mercy sustain us through all that we have to suffer. We do pray, Lord, for protection, for wisdom, for leadership, and also for discernment in the small things for Jesus Christ, Lord."

Today we have an interesting selection of readings for the fourth Sunday in Lent. I often quarrel with the lectionary because of the use of the Old Testament readings. I don't really like the way that the stories are chopped up. The older lectionary had the Old Testament lessons speaking directly to the New Testament lessons. And I must say I preferred that. But on the other hand, when you have an experience like the experience I've had these last couple of days in researching, reading and researching the story of Saul and David, then I am grateful to be sent back into this extraordinary series of stories in First and Second Samuel.

I once heard a wise preacher on the radio say that he never preached from a text unless he first read the whole book from which the text came. That's asking quite a lot in the case of Jeremiah or Ezekiel, but I have found it to be very wise counsel. And so I read not only the story for today, which is familiar to many people, but also the stories surrounding it both before and after in 1 and 2 Samuel, a most extraordinary collection of stories about the kingdom of Israel and its leaders.

And so, I'm going to read the passage reported for today from the Revised Standard Version, my favorite.

This is the sixteenth chapter of the first book of the prophet Samuel. The Israelites' king, Saul, has just committed a grievous sin against God in chapter 15, one which gives great trouble to modern people, and I'll talk about that later. But you need to know that this event in chapter 16 is preceded by the Lord's decision to reject Saul as the future king and leader of Israel. This grieves the prophet Samuel because he had trained Saul for this role and is quite devastated by what has happened.

But the Lord said to Samuel, how long will you grieve over Saul? Seeing that I have rejected him from being king over Israel, fill your horn with oil and go. I will send you to Jesse. the Bethlehemite, for I have provided for myself a king among his sons. And Samuel said, how can I go? If Saul hears this, he will kill me. And the Lord said, take a heifer with you and say, I have come to sacrifice the Lord and invite Jesse to the sacrifice. And I will show you what you shall do. And you shall anoint for me him whom I name to you.

Samuel did what the Lord
commanded and came to Bethlehem.
The elders of the city came to meet
Samuel trembling and said, do you
come peaceably? And he said,
peaceably, I have come to sacrifice
to the Lord. Consecrate yourselves
and come with me to the sacrifice.
And he consecrated Jesse and his
sons and invited them to come to the
sacrifice. When they came, he
looked on Eliab, the oldest son, and
he thought, surely the Lord's
anointed stands before me. But the
Lord said to Samuel, do not look on
his appearance or on the height of his
stature, because I have rejected him.
For the Lord sees not as man sees.
Man looks on the outward
appearance, but the Lord looks on
the heart. Then Jesse called
Abinadab and made him pass before
Samuel. And the Lord said, neither
have I chosen this one.

Then Jesse made Shammel pass by
and he said, neither has the Lord
chosen this one. And Jesse made
seven of his sons pass before
Samuel. And Samuel said to Jesse,

the Lord has not chosen these. And
Samuel said to Jesse, are all your
sons here? And he said, there
remains yet the youngest, but behold,
he is keeping the sheep. And Samuel
said to Jesse, send and fetch him, for
we will not set down until he comes
here. And so Jesse sent and brought
him in. Now David was ruddy and
had beautiful eyes and was
handsome. And the Lord said, arise,
anoint him, for this is he. Then
Samuel took the horn of oil and
anointed David in the midst of his
brothers. And the spirit of the Lord
came mightily upon David from that
day forward.

And Samuel rose up and went to
Rama, and the Spirit of the Lord
departed from Saul.

May the Lord bless this reading of His holy
word.

Now, this is a very well-known story, and
there's a verse in it, which I'm sure many of
you recognize, that is very often quoted,
"The Lord sees not as man sees. Man looks

on the outward appearance, but the Lord looks on the heart." Today we would say the Lord sees not as a human being sees. A human being looks on the outward appearance, but the Lord looks on the heart.

Most people preaching and teaching this passage today will emphasize that particular saying and will use it in contemporary situations, perhaps to encourage someone who's uncomfortable about his appearance or perhaps because of someone who is feeling insecure or someone who is wondering if the Lord has something special for him to do or for her to do. In other words, such a preacher isolates this verse from its context. Well, that's not wrong exactly because this is a true saying and worthy of all men to be received, but isolating it from its context really does fail to do justice to this extraordinary weaving together of texts about Saul and David and about the prophetic role of Samuel in Israel.

I think it's a joke in a way because as it turns out, David is not probably tall. What emerges, I think, from the text and especially the Goliath story, is that David is apparently somewhat slight in appearance compared to his big brothers and certainly

compared to Goliath. But we also should
know that David's brothers looked down on
him. We learn this later in the story. It's very
much like the elder brothers of Joseph, who
were very contemptuous of Joseph, as we
know from that story, and wish him harm.
Well, the same is true to some extent of the
elder brothers of David.

They can't believe that this stripling who has
been keeping the sheep all these months and
perhaps years has been called forth over
them. The fact that David is a shepherd, of
course, is extremely important. The image of
the shepherd pervades the prophetic works
of the Bible and particularly, I think of
Ezekiel in which the role of the shepherd,
Good Shepherd and the Wicked Shepherd is
emphasized, and the sheep are the people
Israel. We're all used to this from the Psalms
and from the prophets and from Jesus
himself who casts himself in the role of the
Good Shepherd. And so the fact that David
as a boy, and he really is nothing more than
a boy here (How old? Maybe sixteen,
something like that.) All these months and
perhaps years, this shepherd boy is being
groomed by God to be the leader of Israel,
but not only the leader of Israel, but to be
the progenitor of the line from which the

Messiah will descend. And so the shepherd figure takes on enormous importance.

And yet, in understanding who David is, we need to think of him as a solitary figure out in the fields with these dumb and stupid sheep to take care of. And of course, sheep are not necessarily all that dumb and stupid. That's kind of a caricature that we have that we love to emphasize when we talk about sheep. But in fact, it's the dependence of sheep, the need of sheep for care that is important in discussing shepherds and sheep in the context of Israel and the people of God. The shepherd is responsible for caring for the sheep and for making sure that they are not prey to wolves or other predators. David has been out in the fields by himself a great deal carrying out this task. And one of the old commentators, which are so valuable, that I read in preparation for this talk, pointed out that, assuming that David had something to do with the writing of the psalms, we don't really know how much. But let's follow the tradition and say that these psalms that I'm about to point out are indeed psalms of David. This old preacher points out that Psalm 8 is this splendid nighttime vision that might have been seen by a shepherd in the field:

Lord our God.

How majestic is thy name in all the earth. When I look at the heavens, the works of thy hands, the moon and the stars which thou hast established, what is man that thou art mindful of him and the son of man that thou dost care for him? Yet thou hast made him little less than God and dost crown him with glory and honor. Thou hast given him dominion over the works of thy hands and has put all things under his feet. O Lord our God, how majestic is thy name in all the earth. The nighttime vision of a shepherd who will ultimately come to be crowned with glory and honor. And then the old preacher says that the shepherd moves on from there to his daytime vision. in the fields, the heavens declare the glory of God and the firmament proclaims his handiwork. In the heavens he has set a tent for the sun, which comes forth like a bridegroom leaving his chamber, and like a strong man runs its course with joy. Its rising is from the end of the heavens and its circuit to the end of them, and there is nothing hid from its heat. We can perhaps think of the young shepherd seeing the sunrise and move across the heavens in his daytime work.

I think the thought of David being prepared to understand the majesty and glory of God, culminating of course with Psalm 23, is a lovely one. I don't need to read Psalm 23, because everyone knows Psalm 23, the shepherd's song. But as we think about David and his calling, it's lovely to be reminded by this preacher of olden time of how shepherds, how David was a shepherd and was being formed in his heart for God as he was out in the fields by himself from the time he was a child.

Now, the stories about Saul and David are extraordinary in their political importance, and that makes them even more relevant to today. When we take a saying like, "God looks not on the outward appearance, but on the heart," that is cited in a political context because what's happening here is that the ruler of Israel, the country, the nation, the people is being chosen, and he will become the greatest king that Israel ever had, but also at the same time, the greatest sinner. I'd like to point out that I've gone through all kinds of books that treat this passage, and I saved Karl Barth for the end, which I always do. That was a big mistake because I did not know that Karl Barth wrote an entire section called "The Elect and the Rejected." This is part of the big section of that section, and in it he has a so-called footnote, the small print, which goes for something like fifty pages. It's all about Saul and David, the rejected and the elected. Saul is rejected; David is elected.

Now what does this mean for us? Let's get the context of the whole story here. I can't give the full context, because it's forty pages long. But just to think about what goes before and after this one passage, when you read the whole two books, 1 and 2 Samuel, you see that this is not just a little isolated story about how nice it is that God looks at our hearts and not our appearance. That would leave us thinking, "Ooh, what's the state of my heart? Maybe the state of my heart is not good enough." Or we might conversely think, "Well, my heart's in a good state, so I don't really need to worry about how I look or how I behave or anything else of that nature, that outward nature, that's not important. What's really important is the state of my heart, which leads to the question, how is the state of my heart vis-a-vis God?" That, to me, is a very anxiety-producing question.

All right, now let's look at the story in detail.
First of all, we notice that Samuel is in deep
grief about the failure of his protege, Saul. I
have to mention what has happened to Saul,
because it causes modern people an
enormous amount of trouble. Saul has been
commanded to wipe the Amalekites off the
face of the earth, basically. He has been told
that he is going to be given victory over the
Amalekites who have caused no end of
trouble and suffering for the people of Israel.
We have to realize that the Israelites has
experienced suffering and death and
deprivation over a period of time caused by
the Amalekites. God commands his
appointed king, Saul (his chosen king) , to
take a troop of thousands and thousands out
and slaughter the Amalekites (all of them,
including babies and sucklings), and to kill
all the animals and leave nothing behind.
This causes serious problems for us. Samuel
doesn't obey this command. First we think
that Saul is a great humanitarian, because he
doesn't want to do away with all the
Amalekite people, including the babies and
women, and he is merciful. Saul preserves
the life of the king of the Amalekites, and
his soldiers pick out all the animals that look
good to them and take them off to preserve
and presumably use themselves or make
other use of in their own families and in

their own farms. And so the Lord is wrathful against Saul, because Saul has disobeyed God. Now I was really struggling with this because it seems as if Saul actually disobeys God in order to be merciful to the Amalekites.

But it turns out that this is not the ancient way of looking at this story. We have to see it through the ways in which those who first read it would have understood it. First of all, it is clear on second reading that the animals are not killed out of mercy to the animals, but because the animals are useful. Soldiers can carry them off and make use of them. It's very clear from the story that it's selfish and it's to their profit, because they take the animals and do not kill them.

But what about not taking the king and preserving his life instead? Well, for one thing, the king could have been held for ransom. That's another factor that I wouldn't have thought of. In any case, again, as one of the old preachers says, what's at stake here is whether God ultimately has the right of life and death. The question is whether God is the rightful judge over his people and whether he has the right of judgment and mercy? Now, some of the old commentators speak here about the Old Dispensation and the New Dispensation. And we have to be careful about that language because it can cause anti-Semitic attitudes. And we do need to be careful about it, but I don't think we can do away with it altogether, because we do read the Old Testament through the lens of Christian faith. And when we read a passage like this about the Amalekites, we ask ourselves, "Is this the last word about God? Is this what God really wants in light of Jesus Christ?" And I think we have to say no.

But at the same time, we need to respect the way in which this text was originally put together in which it poses the question of who ultimately has the right of judgment or mercy, who ultimately makes the decisions about life and death. And that, to be sure, is a question that we ask this very day as we learn of people whom we personally know who have been tested positive for the coronavirus. My own grandson is being tested now. And I have just heard of others who have been tested positive, and it cuts very close. And so the question arises for us, who ultimately is the Lord of Death and the Lord of Life? This was a very, very close question for the ancient peoples, because they lived with death all the time in a way that we don't.

There's a hymn that I must say affects me deeply every time I sing it. It's not in the Episcopal hymn book, but I'm deeply touched by it all the time. It's called, *Dear, Jesus, I Love Thee*: "If ever I love thee, it is now. If ever I love thee, Jesus, it is now." That's the chorus. And in its verses it speaks of a person's life. It follows this with a verse about the death of the person who's saying this, describing loving Jesus in this way, "When death due is on my brow, if ever I love thee, Jesus, it is now." And I understand that there's a tradition that this text was written by a boy of sixteen. I thought that text couldn't possibly have written by a boy that age. A boy of 16 is not thinking about death. He's never seen death due on the forehead of a dying person. And then I thought, yes, he has, because he was in the nineteenth century when family members died at home. A sixteen-year-old certainly saw it.

My own great-grandfather Eugene Davis was sixteen when his father was shot dead at the University of Virginia (true story), and he sat by his father's bedside as his father died. He saw the death due on his father's brow. And later as a Christian man who was converted to Christ, Eugene Davis knew what it meant to say, "If ever I saw thee, if ever I loved thee, Jesus, it is now," because his father's death was followed by both his son and his daughter dying young.

The boy of sixteen who saw his father die also saw his daughter and son die in their twenties, and yet Eugene Davis in his old age spoke of a prayer answering God.

Now why am I off on this subject? It's because reading the context of the story about David reminds me that the issue is who has the right of life and death? Who has the right of judgment and mercy? Who has the right to reject a leader and anoint a new leader? The answer to that can only be Almighty God, the King of Israel, the God and Father of our Lord Jesus Christ. But we're reading this through the eyes of one who has seen and known the Lord Jesus Christ. with considerable help from Karl Barth, we are able to see Saul and David as the elect and the rejected. Saul as the rejected one, David as the elect one, Beyond that we see Jesus Christ as the one who becomes the rejected one for our sakes, that we all may be the elect. And what that all means is not clear. I'm way ahead of myself here, but this is the way my mind starts going when I'm deeply into a text like this. What a blessing that is.

I think of what Paul says, using the word *all,* "In Adam, all die, even so in Christ, all shall be made alive. God has consigned all human beings to disobedience in order that he may have mercy upon all." Now David Bentley Hart has used those two verses from Paul's epistles in his new book about whether or not we are to believe in universal salvation. The answer, I think, to that question always has to be that we don't know. But there is a suggestion in Paul's use of the word *all* in the context specifically of the elect and the rejected, that leaves the way open to hope, at least, that there is a way for all. But that is only a hope, and our ultimate hope is in God, who alone has the right to administer justice and mercy and to decide between life and death. Clearly, the story of Saul and the story of David prefigures God's decision in Christ to become both Saul and David in himself, to be the one who was rejected and to be the one who was elected.

So, all of this amazing story in 1 and 2 Samuel, I read just as a story this week. Just read it first as a story. Read it from a modern translation, just as a story, as if you were reading a walloping good adventure tale. And it is that. But then read it again and see what strikes you theologically and why these stories were put together the way that they are.

Let me go back now. The Lord is very crisp with Samuel, his prophet. Samuel is a very old man at this point. This is an example of the wholeness of the Bible. Every child should know the story of little Samuel who is taken by his mother, dedicated at the temple and given to the prophet Eli, who is a mess and his family is a mess— speaking of the mercy of God and the wonder of God working through flawed human beings. Eli's whole household is corrupt, and yet Eli is the one who brings up little Samuel. And when the God calls Samuel in the night, "Samuel, Samuel," the boy goes to Eli, who is relatively clueless, and says, "I heard a voice." Eli says, "go back to bed." This happens three times. The third time Samuel goes to Eli, Eli says something to this effect, "Samuel, I think God is calling you. Go back to bed, but listen to what he has to say." And what God has to say is the downfall of the host of Eli.

That's a pretty strong message to give to a little child to deliver, but it becomes very important in the later story of Israel. Samuel grows up to be the protege of Eli and comes to understand his utter dependence upon God. He goes through many, many trials and grows up to become the great prophet of Israel and wins respect and awe. He is called upon to anoint Saul and to raise up Saul as a worthy king. Saul fails, because Saul does not understand that only God has the right to decide who is to live and who is to die. That's really the theological point. And Samuel is grief stricken by the downfall of his beloved pupil, the one whom he has groomed to be the king over all God's people.

But God says to Samuel in chapter 16, the text for today, "Samuel, I'm tired of waiting for you to get over your grief. I've got something for you to do. I've got something for you to do, Samuel. Fill your horn with oil."

Gregory the Great a Roman pope in the late sixth century. said a wonderful thing, which is not the kind of thing that modern preachers are used to saying, because we don't think this way. Gregory the Great said that when God told Samuel, "quit, quit crying over Saul, get up, fill your horn with oil and go…" the fullness of the horn refers to the perseverance of grace. Isn't that wonderful? The perseverance of God's grace in spite of the failure of the anointed one.

And then Samuel says, "I can't go. If Saul hears about this, he will kill me." And the Lord says, "No, I've got a scheme here. You take a heifer and go to Jesse in Bethlehem and say, 'I have come to sacrifice to the Lord.' That will protect you, Samuel."

This old prophet just walking down the road towing a heifer with one hand and carrying the oil in the other hand. Wonderful picture!

This must have brought a great deal of fear and trembling to Jesse, or maybe excitement. We don't know how Jesse felt, but Jesse is picked out by the great prophet to go to this special sacrifice. So Samuel goes to Jesse with the heifer and the full horn of oil, presumably taking great care of not spill any of it. And he came to Bethlehem, and the elders of the city came to meet Samuel trembling. Why are they trembling? It is because they sense that Samuel has come in judgment. They know that Samuel, being the Lord's prophet, has the right of judgment. So they say, "are you coming in judgment or are you coming in peace?" And Samuel says, "I'm coming in peace. I have come to sacrifice to the Lord. Come with me to the sacrifice."

And so Jesse and his sons were consecrated and came to the sacrifice.

Then Samuel goes through the procedure in today's passage. These strapping young men appear before him, and their height is emphasized. The older brothers are very tall, big men. That's emphasized. It's their size rather than their handsomeness, I think, that we want to focus on. And Samuel is perplexed because God rejects all of the big fellows. He says, "Jesse, are all of your sons here?" And Jesse, "Of course." He says, "well, the youngest one is out keeping the sheep." And Samuel says, "go and fetch him." And Jesse brought him in and he was handsome.

David is the sexiest guy in the Bible, I always like to say. But he wasn't particularly big. I think we can conclude that from the stories that we hear later. David was imposing in appearance but not big. Therefore he presented quite a contrast to Goliath a couple of chapters later. But he was handsome, and the Lord said, anoint him, this is he. And Samuel took the horn of oil and anointed him in the midst of his brothers, the jealous brothers. And the spirit of the Lord came mightily upon David from that day forward.

That's the important line. The Spirit of God descended mightily upon David from that day forward. And that's really important, because we have to remember that David was not only the author of those beautiful Psalms, the daytime one and the nighttime one, but he is also the author, so to speak of the Psalm for Ash Wednesday, Psalm 51, which is by any measure the most thoroughgoing passage in the Bible of personal repentance of sin.

I'm not going to read the whole thing, but it begins, "Have mercy on me, O God, according to thy abundant mercy."

(That's that full horn of oil.) "Thy abundant mercy, wash me thoroughly from my sin, for I know my transgressions and my sin is ever before me, so that thou art justified in thy sentence and blameless in thy judgment." That is the cry of a man who truly knows the depth of his own sinfulness and who also at the same time knows what his relationship to God is and how it is God who stands ready to clean his heart. This is the man about whom we read in 1 Samuel. This is the man whose whose heart God looks upon and chooses. But this heart is very defective. David does not stand before God in his adulthood and say, "Look, Lord, you chose me on account of my heart." He says instead, "Create in me a clean heart, O God, and put a new and right spirit within me. Cast me not from thy presence and take not thy Holy Spirit from me."

And that's in the context, you see, of God having chosen David because he looked on his heart and that God's Spirit came upon David mightily, and yet David is reduced to saying, "Cast not thy Holy Spirit from me." Only you, O God, can clean my heart and put a new and right spirit within me. That's the prayer that the whole church prays on Ash Wednesday.

Let's return to the whole idea of the elect and the rejected. There isn't any human being who has ever been born who has not deserved rejection by God in some way. That's clear in the scripture. There isn't a single person in the scripture, certainly not the great King David of all people, who can consider himself or herself free of any need to submit to the judgment of God. But it is in this section that Karl Barth has written about David and Saul, it is this particular section in which Barth comes to say things like this.

"Well," he says, "the King of Israel rejected by God, and that would be Saul and would have been David." The King of Israel rejected by God is the prototype and copy of Jesus Christ. And that's what we see on the cross. We see the one rejected by God. How awesome that is. Nothing in Christian theology could be more awesome to say. The king of Israel rejected by God is the prototype and copy of Jesus Christ. But he says also that the act of God's grace, which took place when David was anointed out of that full horn, possesses and retains the character of an act of judgment. The act of grace retains the character of an act of judgment.

Because the man in whom God has entered
upon his kingdom as a kingdom of grace for
all his people is always the very one whom
God has rejected for the sin of the whole
people. I don't know about you all, I've
become quite overcome by in-depth study of
scripture. And I don't get to do it as often as
I would like now because I don't teach
anymore in a steady way or preach in a
steady way, which is a of a deprivation. You
are very fortunate you are in a Bible study
that meets regularly with the same people, or
if you're a preacher, because you are
required really by the rhythms of your life to
be deeply immersed in Scripture all the time,
and to see these links within a story so full
of horror and unworthiness and bad behavior
and selfishness and greed and corruption. It's
a strange new world of revival, as Barth
says, a world in which all this badness goes
on, seemingly without any constraint. And
yet there is this action of God in judgment,
like the judgment upon Saul. And the story
of Saul is not pretty, particularly since he
began so spectacularly well. Tall Saul,
unlike small David, which is interesting.
When Saul was anointed, the people poured
out into the streets and said they had never
seen such a magnificent king. But David,
who danced before the Lord in nothing but a
jockstrap, committed a sin which,

interestingly, Barth says was worse than the sin of Saul: deliberately murdering his paramour's husband. That's pretty bad. But in any case, whether it was worse or not, we have here two people, Saul and David, both of whom violated the trust that had been placed in them by God. One of them dies a wretched death. The other one reigns over Israel in a glorious story which becomes emblematic of the whole history of Israel. His death is kind of sad too. Not as sad as Saul's, but sad, a story of infirmity — pathetic really, David's death.

So, this whole thing is about life and death in a way. Saul dies essentially without being shriven. He does not fall on his knees and pray the fifty-first psalm. And yet it seems to me Saul played his role in Israel's story as the one who is rejected and David, the self-admitted miserable sinner, plays his role as the one who is chosen and anointed.

This is the story of all of us because Jesus Christ has taken election and rejection into himself. And this means that he has taken all of us into himself. Though it is not the reading for the day, Romans 11 brings us into this. It is the deepest place in the New Testament. I choose the word deep deliberately. I don't say it's the best passage or the most grace-filled passage or the most spectacular passage or the most revealing of Jesus passage or whatever. still looking for it. I say it's the deepest.

And I mean the deepest because I think it probes most deeply into the future of the human race and the way in which judgment and grace figure in the future. Paul is struggling with the unbelief of the Jewish people. He expected them to come running to Jesus the Messiah and they haven't. And he's in anguish about it. And he talks about his anguish for three chapters. And finally, he concludes that it's all part of God's plan. That he has rejected some, , Saul, for instance, in order that he might use another, let's say, David, for the ultimate redemption of everyone. Now, I'm not saying that as a certainty any more than Paul is, but I'm saying it as something that faith and hope lead us to envision, because all things are possible with God. But whether we believe or can say without doubt that everyone's gonna be saved in the end, we should never say that lightly or easily or self-righteously:

   "Because I'm such a big-hearted person and am so inclusive, I can therefore say everybody's going to be included. Jesus has taught me to be inclusive so I can therefore say everybody will be included."

But that's making God very small. We have to continue to confess that it is God who has the right of life and death. It is God who will decide about judgment and grace. And if indeed we seem to see in Jesus Christ the triumph, ultimately, of grace over judgment, nevertheless, judgment is part of the story. Saul is part of the story, just as David is, and judgment upon David is part of the story. And it is in Jesus Christ that we see this, the elect and the rejected. And so Paul comes to the end of the three chapters devoted to this problem of the unbelief of the people that he expected to believe. And he says, "lest you be wise in your own conceits." See, that's our problem.

We are wise in our own conceits. Maybe we're wise because we believe in the inclusivity of God, or maybe we're wise because we think we know better than to believe in the inclusivity of God. Maybe we think we've got the answer to that because we know that God does not judge people. I'm just caricaturing here, but I'm trying to show that all of us are subject to this kind of minimizing of God's power. We want to make the decisions and not give the decision to God. And so, Paul says, lest you be wise in your own conceits, I want you to understand this mystery, brothers and sisters. A hardening has come upon part of Israel. That is to say, there are some people who just don't seem to believe and don't seem are ever going to be believers. And that includes, in some cases, your grandchildren and mine, we just don't understand why some people just don't seem to believe. But lest you be wise in your own conceits, brothers and sisters, God is the one who is in charge of this:

> A hardening has come upon part of Israel until the full number of the Gentiles comes in and then all Israel will be saved as it is written. As it is written, the deliverer will come from Zion. He will come from Zion. He will come from within Israel. And he will banish ungodliness from Jacob. And this will be my covenant with them when I take away their sins. that's in the future, you see. As regards for the gospel, unbelievers, enemies, are enemies of God, but they are enemies of God for your sake.

As regards election, they are beloved for the sake of their forefathers, David being one of them, of course. For the gifts and the call of God are irrevocable. That's good news for David and it's good news for Saul. Just as you, you believers, that's you and me.

Just as you believers were once disobedient to God, but have now received mercy because of the disobedience of Saul, let's say, disobedience of failed people, disobedient to unfaithful, unbelieving people, they have been disobedient in order that by the mercy shown to you, they also may receive mercy. For God has consigned all human beings to disobedience, that he may have mercy upon all. the depth of the riches and wisdom and knowledge of God. How unsearchable are his judgments and how inscrutable his ways. Who has known the mind of the Lord? Who has been his counselor? Who has given a gift to God in order that he or she might be repaid from him and through him and to him are all things. To him be glory forever. Amen.

Now that's Romans 11. That's the climax of the preaching of Paul, the teaching of Paul. We might say it is the climax of the entire theological project of the Bible. And Saul and David fit right into that in a way that I had never seen before. Grace and mercy contain judgment. Judgment is held in suspension, so to speak. I don't really know anything about chemistry, but I imagine a liquid in suspension. Judgment is suspended within grace.

And therefore, we do not need to fear the judgment because we are already held by the grace of God. But if we despise the idea of judgment and think that we can sweep away judgment by some statement such as, God loves everybody or God doesn't judge anybody, that would be seriously to miss the entire biblical story, which culminates, I believe, with the crucifixion of the one who takes upon himself the judgment and the shame and the rejection that belong to us in order that, as Paul says, in order that the rejected may become the elect in Christ.

Now all that comes from studying, in this case, in the case of what's happening right now, all of this comes from studying the story of Saul and David, the one who was rejected by God and the one who was elected. And I guess we can hope for Saul's redemption along with David's, but not without a cost. God does not just go around patting malefactors on the head and saying, "There, there. It's really all right. I don't judge you." That's not what God does. Our need is to be cleaned from the inside out, to be purified in the refiner's fire like fuller's soap. I don't know anything about fulling, but I do know that the kind of soap that fullers use is rough on the skin like lye soap. The process of being justified in Christ is not painless. It's pure gift, but it's not going to come without a stab of understanding that we are unclean, impure, unwashed. This is the washing that happens in baptism. And nothing can undo what God has done. God has consigned everyone to disobedience in order that he may have mercy on all. the majesty and glory and wonder of Christ, the earth declares the glory of God, the heavens declare the glory of God.

And then we go back into the world of death and disease and infection and danger and fear. And it's getting very close. But there isn't anything that God has not already thought of.

One time I was in distress about thinking about dystopia. I don't know whether I just finished reading a dystopian novel or not, but I do like reading dystopian things. I really was quite agitated and went to someone saying "I really have been sort of shaken up by this dystopian thing because I've suddenly began thinking, 'Suppose the last people on earth, the last community on earth is in a moonscape of destroyed earth and there's no bread and no wine and nothing to make bread or wine out of. How can we have communion?'" And my wise elder said, "Fleming, did you think God had not thought of that?" Now maybe that doesn't strike others as the way it struck me, but it lifted me onto another plane of our sight where there is nothing that God has not already thought and nothing that he has not already entered. Nothing that he has not already undergone — they gave him vinegar to drink. There is nothing that God has not thought of, but that he has not redeemed.

And so we do need to take heart and face what the future of the COVID virus holds, the near future in this case. The near future in the United States and Europe and around the world, Asia certainly, Africa maybe. Only Antarctica is free. Should we all move to Antarctica? Well, I'm being silly, but not really, because we need to know, as Jesus said, I have told you all things beforehand.

We need to know that there is nothing that God does not know beforehand. And in that knowledge, only that knowledge, the knowledge that comes to us in Jesus Christ, only in that knowledge can we truly cast out fear. Because love casts that fear and God is love.

Almighty and most merciful God. These days, we are a fearful people. And if we're not a little bit fearful, then we're not facing reality. And so we pray that you would enable us to face reality, human reality, and the reality of an enemy who wants to undo everything you have done in our knowledge of this ruler of this world who has taken advantage of our fall, this adversary who has been set against you almost but not quite from the beginning, that you have already come onto the field of battle and vanquished our adversary, leaving him with his rearguard actions, but arming us with faith and with hope.

Let us wear this armor, dear Lord, not the armor of foolish optimism and careless heedlessness, but with the armor that you have given us by your Spirit and through your word that we may partake of your sacraments in these reduced and truncated circumstances with full knowledge that no disease and not even the greatest of sins has any chance against your redemptive purpose in our Lord Jesus Christ. In His name we pray.

Amen.

Benediction

"Now unto him that is able to keep you from falling, and to present you faultless before the presence of his glory with exceeding joy, To the only wise God our Saviour, be glory and majesty, dominion and power, both now and ever. Amen."

Jude 1:24-25

Meet the Contributors

Jason Micheli is an irreverent reverend, serving as pastor at Annandale United Methodist Church in Annandale, Virginia. He's the author of *A Quid without Any Quo*, *Living in Sin*, and *Cancer Is Funny* and is a henchman behind the Crackers and Grape Juice podcast. He knows scripture, popular culture, church history, and theology — all of which make appearances when you chat with him. He has incurable cancer (see above books) and thinks the lifespan in Psalm 90 sounds pretty good. Above all, he's a grace-hardened sinner whom the gospel of Jesus Christ has conscripted for its own good cause. And he likes pickles.

Teer Hardy is a pastor in the United Methodist Church in Virginia. He co-hosts the Crackers and Grape Juice podcast, stirring up honest conversations about faith, doubt, and the absurd grace of God. When not preaching or podcasting, he's coaching first base, keeping the scorebook, and rehearsing his retirement in the announcer's booth. He believes in grace over grit, good liturgy, and the holiness of a sacrifice bunt. His sermons are short on self-help and long on Jesus. He's raising two kids, drinking too much coffee, and still holding out hope for the Orioles.

Since 2016, **Crackers & Grape Juice** has been bringing you conversations about faith without using stained-glass language. The team is grateful to everyone who has downloaded and supported the podcast over the years.

To learn more about the podcast, visit crackersandgrapejuice.com.

Made in the USA
Middletown, DE
23 June 2025

77396725R00042